First World War
and Army of Occupation
War Diary
France, Belgium and Germany

27 DIVISION
80 Infantry Brigade
Rifle Brigade (The Prince Consort's Own)
4th Battalion
20 December 1914 - 28 October 1915

WO95/2262/2

The Naval & Military Press Ltd
www.nmarchive.com
Published in association with The National Archives

Published by

The Naval & Military Press Ltd

Unit 10 Ridgewood Industrial Park,

Uckfield, East Sussex,

TN22 5QE England

Tel: +44 (0) 1825 749494

www.naval-military-press.com

www.nmarchive.com

This diary has been reprinted in facsimile from the original. Any imperfections are inevitably reproduced and the quality may fall short of modern type and cartographic standards.

© **Crown Copyright**
Images reproduced by permission of The National Archives, London, England, 2015.

Contents

Document type	Place/Title	Date From	Date To
Heading	WO95/2262/2		
Heading	27th Division 80th Infy Bde 4th Bn Rifle Brigade Dec 1914-Oct 1915		
Heading	80th Infantry Brigade. 27th Division (Battn. Disembarked Havre from England 22.12.14) 4th Battn. The Rifle Brigade. December (20 To 31.12.14) 1914		
War Diary	Winchester	20/12/1914	20/12/1914
War Diary	Southampton	21/12/1914	21/12/1914
War Diary	Havre	22/12/1914	23/12/1914
War Diary	Arques	24/12/1914	24/12/1914
War Diary	Blaringhem	25/12/1914	31/12/1914
Heading	80th Infantry Brigade. 27th Division. 4th Battn. The Rifle Brigade. January 1915		
War Diary	Blaringhem	01/01/1915	31/01/1915
Heading	80th Infantry Brigade. 27th Division. 4th Battn. The Rifle Brigade. February 1915		
War Diary		01/02/1915	28/02/1915
Heading	80th Infantry Brigade. 27th Division. 4th Battn. The Rifle Brigade. March 1915		
War Diary		01/03/1915	31/03/1915
Miscellaneous Diagram etc	Appendix I		
Heading	80th Infantry Brigade. 27th Division. 4th Battn. The Rifle Brigade. April 1915		
War Diary		01/04/1915	30/04/1915
Heading	80th Infantry Brigade. 27th Division 4th Battn. The Rifle Brigade. May 1915		
War Diary		01/05/1915	31/05/1915
Heading	80th Infantry Brigade. 27th Division. 4th Battn. The Rifle Brigade. June 1915		
War Diary		01/06/1915	30/06/1915
Heading	80th Infantry Brigade 27th Division. 4th Battn. The Rifle Brigade. July 1915		
War Diary		01/07/1915	31/07/1915
Heading	80th Infantry Brigade. 27th Division. 4th Battn. The Rifle Brigade. August 1915		
War Diary		01/08/1915	29/08/1915
Heading	80th Infantry Brigade 27th Division. 4th Battn. The Rifle Brigade. September 1915		
War Diary		01/09/1915	30/09/1915
Heading	80th Infantry Brigade. 27th Division. 4th Battn. The Rifle Brigade. October 1915		
War Diary		01/10/1915	28/10/1915

WO95/2262/2

27TH DIVISION
80TH INFY BDE

4TH BN RIFLE BRIGADE
DEC 1914 - OCT 1915

80th Infantry Brigade.

27th Division.

(Battn. disembarked
Havre from England
22.12.14)

WAR DIARY

4th BATTN. THE RIFLE BRIGADE.

DECEMBER

(20 to 31.12.14)

1 9 1 4

Army Form C. 2118.

WAR DIARY
or
INTELLIGENCE SUMMARY

(Erase heading not required.)

Instructions regarding War Diaries and Intelligence Summaries are contained in F. S. Regs., Part II. and the Staff Manual respectively. Title pages will be prepared in manuscript.

Hour, Date, Place	Summary of Events and Information	Remarks and references to Appendices
9 am 20.12.14. WINCHESTER	Marched from camp at MAGDALEN HILL to SOUTHAMPTON (14m) Strength 26 Officers (including 1 M.O) 921 other ranks. Arrived 4.30pm embarked on AUSTERLIND.	4M
4pm 21.12.14 SOUTHAMPTON	Sailed	4M
22.12.14 HAVRE	Arrived outside HAVRE 1 am and landed at 2 pm.	4M
23.12.14.	Left Havre 1am. Strength 28 Officers 920 other ranks; One man to Hospital.	4M
24.12.14. ARQUES	Arrived at 2am, & left at 4.30 am and marched to BLARINGHEM about 7 miles. Went into billets	Reference map FRANCE ST. OMER 4

Forms/C. 2118/11.

Army Form C. 2118.

WAR DIARY
or
INTELLIGENCE SUMMARY

(Erase heading not required.)

Instructions regarding War Diaries and Intelligence Summaries are contained in F. S. Regs., Part II. and the Staff Manual respectively. Title pages will be prepared in manuscript.

Hour, Date, Place	Summary of Events and Information	Remarks and references to Appendices
BLARINGHEM 25.12.14.	Xmas day. Three men joined from England, having been absent when the Bn. marched off.	&c.
26.12.14.	Route march and an attack. 1 man to Hospital	&c.
27.12.14.	Digging trenches 1½ miles North of BLARINGHEM	&c.
28.12.14	" "	&c.
	2 men to hospital	&c.
29.12.14	Digging trenches North of BLARINGHEM at LABELLE HOTESSE	
30.12.14	Digging trenches at STEEN BECQUE. 1 man to Hospital	&c.
31.12.14	" "	

Lt. Col. The signs Major J Hasler for + 2 NCOs proceeded to the trenches of the 9th Bde 1st Division

80th Infantry Brigade.
27th Division.

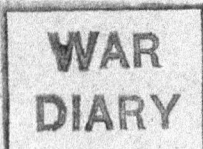

4th BATTN. THE RIFLE BRIGADE.

J A N U A R Y

1 9 1 5

Army Form C. 2118.

WAR DIARY
or
INTELLIGENCE SUMMARY

(Erase heading not required.)

Instructions regarding War Diaries and Intelligence Summaries are contained in F. S. Regs., Part II. and the Staff Manual respectively. Title pages will be prepared in manuscript.

Hour, Date, Place	Summary of Events and Information	Remarks and references to Appendices
BLARINGHEM. 1.1.15	Digging in the morning. Afternoon inspection by the Field Marshal Commanding-in-Chief; Strength on parade 28 Officers (includes M.O.) and 680 other ranks. No machine gun detachments or transport on parade. Party who 10 men reported medically unfit for service. proceeded to the trenches returned to Head Quarters.	A/M
2.1.15.	Digging on 2nd line of trenches in the same place as on 27.12.14 ie 1½ miles N. of BLARINGHEM.	A/M
3.1.15.	Digging. Continuation of work commenced 2.1.15.	A/M
4.1.15.	No digging done; General cleaning up.	1/M
5.1.15.	Marched to METEREN about 13 miles. Strength 28 officers 903 other ranks.	A/M

1217 W 3299 200,000 (L) 8/14 J.B.C. & A. Forms/C. 2118/11.

Army Form C. 2118.

WAR DIARY
or
INTELLIGENCE SUMMARY

(Erase heading not required.)

Instructions regarding War Diaries and Intelligence Summaries are contained in F. S. Regs., Part II. and the Staff Manual respectively. Title pages will be prepared in manuscript.

Hour, Date, Place	Summary of Events and Information	Remarks and references to Appendices
6.1.15.	Marched via DICKEBUSCH to the Trenches and took over Trenches occupied by 3 Companies of the French about 1 mile South of the R in VOORMEZEELE. Lt and QrMr H.E. Worthing admitted to hospital suffering from Hernia.	Reference map. OSTEND I / 100,000 — JMT
7.1.15.	Heavy shelling most of the day, part of Battalion Head Quarters set on fire. Took over Trenches occupied by the remaining French Coy and machine gun.	JMT
8.1.15.	Relieved at night by 2nd K.S.L.I. and moved in support to PLAS ELZONVALLE (3 coys) and 1 Coy at Chateau near KRUISSTRAATHOEK. Casualties in Trenches Killed 2, Wounded 4, Missing 1	JMT
9.1.15.	In support as above.	JMT
10.1.15.	Relieved at night by A and S. Highlanders and marched to DICKEBUSCH.	JMT

WAR DIARY or INTELLIGENCE SUMMARY

Army Form C. 2118.

(Erase heading not required.)

Hour, Date, Place	Summary of Events and Information	Remarks and references to Appendices
11.1.15.	Marched to BOESCHEPE about 8 miles. The men having suffered severely from their feet in the trenches and from want of boots, the march was a considerable tax on their endurance.	J.M.
12.1.15.	In reserve at BOESCHEPE, 100 men admitted to hospital and approximately another 100 men unfit to march.	J.M.
13.1.15.	Marched to DICKEBUSCH	J.M.
14.1.15.	Relieved together with 2/K.S.L.I. the 2/P.C.L.I. Trenches.	J.M.
15.1.15.		J.M.
16.1.15	Relieved by Royal Irish Fusiliers and marched to DICKEBUSCH. Casualties in trenches 1 Killed 1 wounded 3	J.M.
17.1.15	Marched to RENINGHELST in reserve.	J.M.

Army Form C. 2118.

WAR DIARY
or
INTELLIGENCE SUMMARY

(Erase heading not required.)

Instructions regarding War Diaries and Intelligence Summaries are contained in F. S. Regs., Part II. and the Staff Manual respectively. Title pages will be prepared in manuscript.

Hour, Date, Place	Summary of Events and Information	Remarks and references to Appendices
18-1-15.	In reserve.	
19-1-15.	In reserve.	
20-1-15.	In reserve.	
	Battalion State:	
		Officers / O. Ranks
	Strength leaving BARINGHAM	28 / 902
	Wastage	2 / 323
	Present strength	26 / 580
	Detail of Wastage	
	Killed	/ 3
	Wounded	/ 7
	Admitted 15 F.Hosp: (sickness)	1 / 217
	At BOESCHEPE (unfit for duty)	1 / 94
	Missing	/ 2
		2 / 323

Army Form C. 2118.

WAR DIARY
or
INTELLIGENCE SUMMARY

(Erase heading not required.)

Instructions regarding War Diaries and Intelligence Summaries are contained in F. S. Regs., Part II. and the Staff Manual respectively. Title pages will be prepared in manuscript.

Hour, Date, Place	Summary of Events and Information	Remarks and references to Appendices
21-1-15	In reserve	
22-1-15	In reserve	
23-1-15	marched from RENINGHELST to DICKEBUSCH	
24-1-15.	Relieved the 2/D.C.L.I in trenches	
25-1-15	Trenches Capt H.H. Helyar killed and one man killed	
26-1-15.	Relieved in trenches by the 2/D.C.L.I. and marched back to DICKEBUSCH. 2 men died of wounds	
27-1-15	In support at DICKEBUSCH	
28-1-15.	Relieved the 2/D.C.L.I in trenches	
29-1-15	In Trenches. One man killed and one wounded	
30-1-15	Relieved by the Gloucester Regt and marched back to DICKEBUSCH.	
31-1-15	marched from DICKEBUSCH to VOORMOZEELE in close support	

80th Infantry Brigade.

27th Division.

WAR DIARY

4th BATTN. THE RIFLE BRIGADE.

FEBRUARY

1 9 1 5

WAR DIARY or INTELLIGENCE SUMMARY

Army Form C. 2118.

(Erase heading not required.)

Hour, Date, Place	Summary of Events and Information	Remarks and references to Appendices
1.2.15.	In close support VOORMOZEELE. 2 coys being billeted in cellars and "dugouts" and the other two Coys at a Chateau near KRUISSTRAATHOEK. Draft of one officer and 154 other ranks arrived.	
2.2.15.	Took over a new line of trenches at ST ELOI relieving the 2/K.S.L.I. Trenches in a very bad condition.	
3.2.15.	Trenches. One Sergt wounded	
4.2.15.	Relief suspended owing to report from 28th Division that the enemy had broken through their lines. Relief finally carried out 2 am 5.2.15. 2/Lt Gracey and 2/Lt Naylor joined.	
5.2.15.	Marched to huts DICKEBUSCH. Left 5.30 pm and marched to billets RENINGHELST. Owing to further alarmist reports from 28th Division, battalion warned to be in a state of constant readiness during the night	

Army Form C. 2118.

WAR DIARY
or
INTELLIGENCE SUMMARY

(Erase heading not required.)

Instructions regarding War Diaries and Intelligence Summaries are contained in F. S. Regs., Part II. and the Staff Manual respectively. Title pages will be prepared in manuscript.

Hour, Date, Place	Summary of Events and Information	Remarks and references to Appendices
6.2.15	In reserve at RENINGHELST	
7.2.15	ditto Draft of One Officer and 257 other ranks arrived	J.W.R.
8.2.15	In reserve at RENINGHELST	
9.2.15	" "	
10.2.15	Marched to DICKEBUSCH.	
11.2.15	In billets at DICKEBUSCH	
12.2.15	Took over section of trenches from 2/K.S.L.I.	
13.2.15	Trenches. One officer Lt Vincent arrived	
14.2.15	Relief postponed. Enemy captured 4 trenches at ST ELOI. Two men wounded	
15.2.15.	Trenches at ST ELOI retaken. One Officer (Lt J.D Calvert) and 4 men killed and 12 men wounded. Relieved at night by the 2/K.S.L.I. and marched to billets at DICKEBUSCH.	

Forms/C. 2118/11.

Army Form C. 2118.

WAR DIARY
or
INTELLIGENCE SUMMARY

(Erase heading not required.)

Instructions regarding War Diaries and Intelligence Summaries are contained in F. S. Regs., Part II. and the Staff Manual respectively. Title pages will be prepared in manuscript.

Hour, Date, Place	Summary of Events and Information	Remarks and references to Appendices
16.2.15	DICKEBUSCH	
17.2.15	Relieved 2/K.S.L.I. in trenches. 5 officers and 257 other Draft of 69 other ranks arrived. Trenches, one man died of wounds and two others wounded	
18.2.15		
19.2.15	Relieved by 2/K.S.L.I. and marched to DICKEBUSCH. One man killed.	1 off R.B
20.2.15	Billets at DICKEBUSCH	
21.2.15	Marched back to RENINGHELST.	
22.2.15	RENINGHELST. Draft of 20 other ranks arrived	
23.2.15		
24.2.15		

Army Form C. 2118.

WAR DIARY
or
INTELLIGENCE SUMMARY

(Erase heading not required.)

Instructions regarding War Diaries and Intelligence Summaries are contained in F. S. Regs., Part II. and the Staff Manual respectively. Title pages will be prepared in manuscript.

Hour, Date, Place	Summary of Events and Information	Remarks and references to Appendices
25-2-15	RENINGHELST.	
26.2.15	Marched to Huts in DICKEBUSCH.	
27.2.15	Relieved Cameron Highlanders in Trenches at 31-E2O1, casualties 1 Killed and 3 wounded. Since we last occupied these trenches on 2-2-15 Conditions had considerably altered for the worse. The Germans have sapped down to within about 25 yards of two of the trenches	
28.2.15	Trenches. Casualties 4 Killed and 7 wounded.	

80th Infantry Brigade.

27th Division.

WAR DIARY

4th BATTN. THE RIFLE BRIGADE.

MARCH

1915

Attached:

Appendix I.

Army Form C. 2118.

WAR DIARY
or
INTELLIGENCE SUMMARY

(Erase heading not required.)

Instructions regarding War Diaries and Intelligence Summaries are contained in F. S. Regs, Part II. and the Staff Manual respectively. Title pages will be prepared in manuscript.

Hour, Date, Place	Summary of Events and Information	Remarks and references to Appendices
1-3-15.	Relieved in Trenches by 2/K.S.L.I. and marched to DICKEBUSCH. Casualties 8 killed 17 wounded. 1 Officer and 70 other ranks joined.	A/M/L
2-3-15.	DICKEBUSCH	A/M/L
3-3-15	Relieved 2/K.S.L.I. in Trenches	A/M/L
4-3-15.	Trenches. Casualties 3 killed and 8 wounded.	A/M/L
5-3-15.	Relieved by 2/K.S.L.I. in Trenches and marched to DICKEBUSCH. Casualties 1 killed 2/Lt. P.A. Naylor and 9 wounded	A/M/L
6-3-15.	DICKEBUSCH. working party detailed for front line digging on casualties 2 wounded.	A/M/L
7-3-15.	Relieved 2/K.S.L.I. in Trenches	A/M/L
8-3-15.	Trenches. Casualties 5 killed and 4 wounded.	A/M/L
9-3-15.	Relieved by 2/K.S.L.I. in Trenches and marched to DICKEBUSCH. Casualties 3 killed and 3 wounded	A/M/L

Army Form C. 2118.

WAR DIARY
or
INTELLIGENCE SUMMARY
(Erase heading not required.)

Instructions regarding War Diaries and Intelligence Summaries are contained in F. S. Regs., Part II. and the Staff Manual respectively. Title pages will be prepared in manuscript.

Hour, Date, Place	Summary of Events and Information	Remarks and references to Appendices
10-3-15	DICKEBUSCH.	N/Mly
11-3-15	Marched from DICKEBUSCH to rest billets at RENINGHELST.	N/Mly
12-3-15	RENINGHELST under orders to move at short notice. Draft of 30 other ranks joined 11/Mly	N/Mly
13-3-15	RENINGHELST. Draft of one officer and 62 other ranks	N/Mly
14-3-15	RENINGHELST at 7pm received orders to march at once to DICKEBUSCH. Arrived DICKEBUSCH about 9.30 pm, and moved down to Cross roads at KRUISSTRAATHOEK after waiting about 1 hour moved into VOORMOZEELE arriving here at 2 A.M. 15.3.15.	N/Mly
15-3-15	Counter attack delivered against the Germans at St ELOI by 2nd R. Bde unsuccessful. At about 3 am orders received to attack the mound. For account of attack see attached report marked I. Casualties Killed. Major A. M. King. Wounded. Capt. H. B. Moslyn Pryce Capt. H. B. Selby Smyth. 2/Lt. R. C. Hargreaves. 2/Lt. G. J. Stoddart. 2/Lt. L. R. Dunne 2/Lt. L. D. Davies " C. Saunders and 2/Lt. T. Willis 16 men killed. and 4 + 16 men killed. 62 men wounded. Missing 2/Lt. T. P. A. Ritchie 5 + and 17 men.	Appendix I. Report on attack on St ELOI and mound. Author Col. G. H. Thesiger C.B. C.M.G.

92nd

Army Form C. 2118.

WAR DIARY
or
INTELLIGENCE SUMMARY
(Erase heading not required.)

Instructions regarding War Diaries and Intelligence Summaries are contained in F. S. Regs., Part II. and the Staff Manual respectively. Title pages will be prepared in manuscript.

Hour, Date, Place	Summary of Events and Information	Remarks and references to Appendices
15-3-15.	After attack marched back to DICKEBUSCH less "D" Coy who were holding R.B. Trench.	H/held
16-3-15.	DICKEBUSCH. Working parties digging trenches SE E201 one man wounded. D Coy relieved in R.B. trench by D.C.L.I.	H/held Sqr
17-3-15.	" " " " " 1 man "	H/held
18-3-15.	Relieved 2/K.S.L.I. in trenches.	H/held
19-3-15.	Trenches. Casualties 1 man killed and 4 wounded. Some trenches taken over by 2nd Royal Scots 3rd Division	H/held
20-3-15.	Relieved by 2/K.S.L.I. in trenches. Casualties 1 killed and 2 wounded.	H/held
21-3-15.	Moved up to VOORMEZEELE and KRUISSTRAATHOEK chateau 1/2 Coys in each place. D Coy being left at DICKEBUSCH. Draft of 120 other ranks joined.	H/held
22-3-15.	Relieved 2/K.S.L.I. in trenches. 30 other ranks rejoined from Composite Battalion at BOESCHEPE	H/held
23-3-15.	Trenches. Casualties one man wounded. Very much less activity shown by the enemy than previously	H/held
24-3-15.	Relieved by 7th Fusiliers 3rd Division and marched back to billets about 1½ miles S.E. of POPERINGHE	H/held

Army Form C. 2118.

WAR DIARY
or
INTELLIGENCE SUMMARY

(Erase heading not required.)

Instructions regarding War Diaries and Intelligence Summaries are contained in F. S. Regs., Part II. and the Staff Manual respectively. Title pages will be prepared in manuscript.

Hour, Date, Place	Summary of Events and Information	Remarks and references to Appendices
25-3-15	Arrived in billets about 3.30 am.	W/July
26-3-15	Billets at above place	W/July
27-3-15	" " " "	W/July
28-3-15	" " " " Draft of 8 officers and one man joined.	W/July
29-3-15	" " " " Draft of 1 officer and 68 other ranks.	W/July
30-3-15	" " " "	
31-3-15	" " " "	
	Names of officers joined during month	
	1st March Capt. G. Watts	
	13th " 2/Lt C.M. Dyer	
	28th " Capt. J.H.A Wallaston	
	" Lt. Q. H Pelham Burn	
	" 2/Lt. Henderson	
	" 2/Lt. Trevelyan	
	" 2/Lt. Duff	
	" 2/Lt. Durrant	
	" 2/Lt. Cortsabadie	
	" 2/Lt. Fairfax-Lucy	

G. Thorpe Col
Comm 4/B.R./15 Brigade

A P P E N D I X   I.

Appendix I

18

Report of night attack on the mound carried out by 4/8th Rifle Bde on the early morning of the 15th.

About 3am, I received orders to attack the Mound. The P.P.C.L.I. being ordered to co-operate on my left and to attack the mound from the EAST of ST ELOI-YPRES road. My information at this time pointed to the fact that the R.B. and K.S.L.I. trench were not held by either side.

I moved out immediately from VOORMOZEELE and halted with the head of the column near the BUS HOUSE to allow the P.P.C.L.I. to get up on my left.

As the P.P.C.L.I. were blocked in VOORMOZEELE and as it would have been light in about an 1½ hours time, I decided to go on; as I moved on the P.P.C.L.I. moved into the fields on my left.

About this time I received a message saying that the R.B. and K.S.L.I. trenches were occupied by the Germans, ~~were~~. An Officer, I think of the Royal Irish, who had been up at ST ELOI, reported that it was impossible to get beyond the bus in front of S4.

The situation was so uncertain and information so vague that I could not issue any definite orders, until I have moved on with a view to ascertaining what the situation was. I therefore moved on with my battalion to a fallen tree on the road in front of S.9 having left one company in reserve at BUS HOUSE. On arrival there heavy fire was opened from my right front, presumably from R.B. trench. I immediately ordered one company under Captain H.B. Mostyn Pryce to attack the R.B. trench, previously warning S.9. that they were going to do so. The next company under Captain W.B. Selby Smyth was ordered to move up the road by platoons and rush the mound. I had to give about 4 hours to allow Captain Mostyn Pryce to deploy his company and it was about 4.40 a.m. before the first platoon moved up the road.

They were heavily fired from Barricade A and from houses and it was reported that all except 4 men had been either killed or wounded including Capt Selby Smyth and 2/Lt. C. Saunders.

I then ordered the remainder of the company to rush Barricade A which they did. In the meantime a report came in from Captain Mostyn Pryce saying that he had occupied the R.B. trench.

After taking Barricade A fire was opened on us from Barricade B and the adjacent houses, so I sent back for the next company under Lt. Stopford Sackville to attack Barricade B, which they did, and also cleared the houses.

Machine Gun fire was now opened from the mound and from another place which I cannot locate, and also heavy RIFLE fire from

Barricade D. Repeated efforts were made by individual officers and men to rush forward, but the sting had gone out of the attack and it was very difficult to bring any more men up owing to the congestion on the road. I however sent back for the company left at the BUS HOUSE, and two companies of the K.S.L.I. under Major Bayley 2/K.S.L.I. reported to me. I ordered him to try and rush the mound. The reserve company which I had sent back for could not get up owing to the block on the road. It was now almost broad daylight, and there was a confused mass of troops by the ST ELOI cross roads, and I decided, that as any combined rush appeared out of the question, to retire. A few men had worked round through the houses on both sides of the road, but any organised advance on these lines was impossible owing to the debris and state of the ground. I consider that the failure of the attack on the mound was mainly due to the following causes.

 1. Want of accurate information owing to lack of time.

 2. The impossibility of making any reconnaissance.

 3. The fact that more than 50% of the Battalion is composed of men of the new army who are not sufficiently trained

21

and disciplined to undertake such a difficult task as this proved to be.

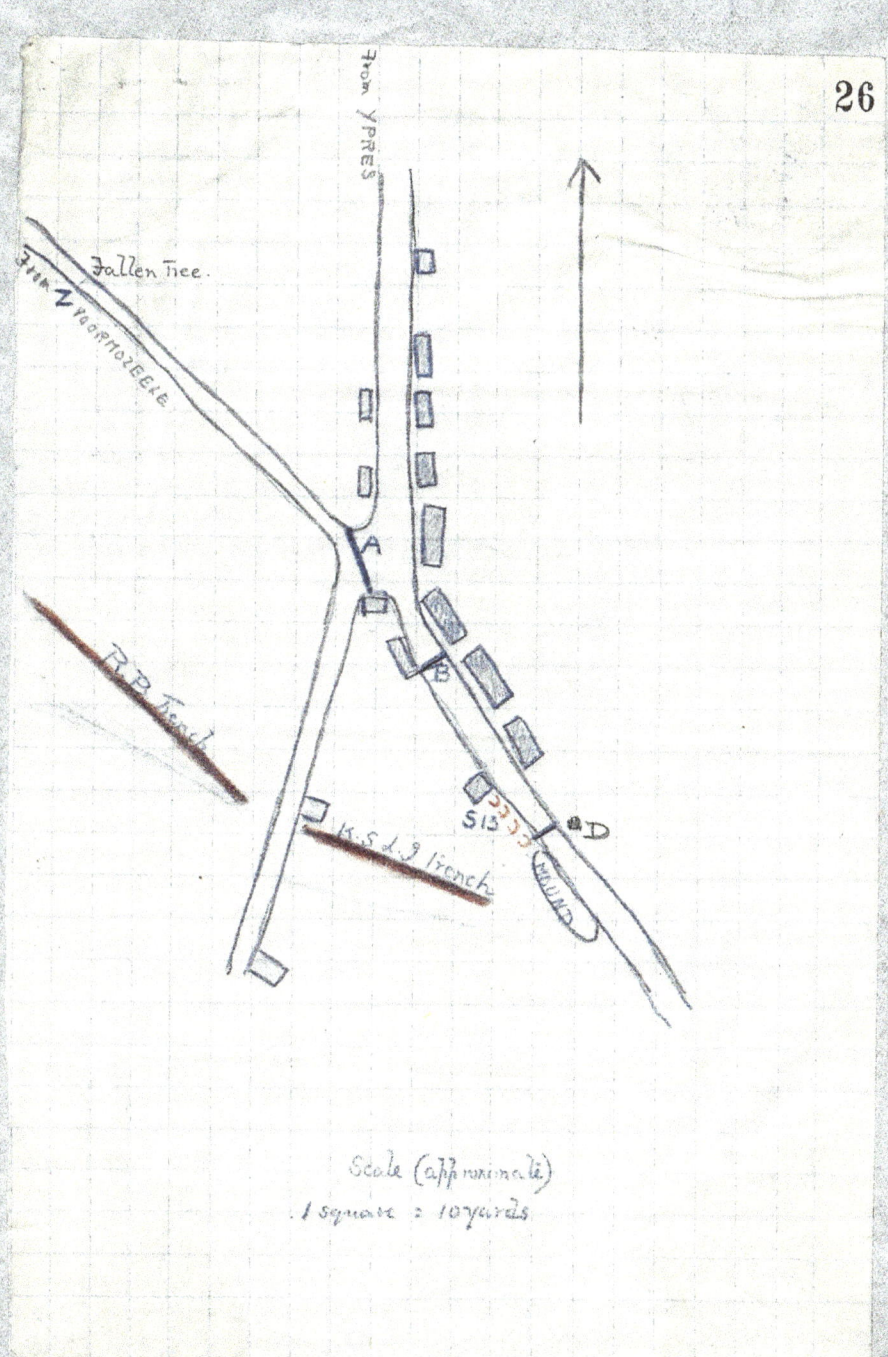

80th Infantry Brigade.

27th Division.

4th BATTN. THE RIFLE BRIGADE.

A P R I L

1 9 1 5

Army Form C. 2118.

WAR DIARY
or
INTELLIGENCE SUMMARY

(Erase heading not required.)

Instructions regarding War Diaries and Intelligence Summaries are contained in F. S. Regs., Part II. and the Staff Manual respectively. Title pages will be prepared in manuscript.

Hour, Date, Place	Summary of Events and Information	Remarks and references to Appendices
1-4-15	Still in huts 1½ miles SE of POPERINGHE	JMS
2-4-15	As above	JMS
3-4-15	As above	JMS
4-4-15	As above	JMS
5-4-15	Marched to YPRES 6 am. Huts there. Officers went to see trenches (in POLYGONE WOOD) which we are taking over from the French.	JMS
6-4-15	In huts at YPRES	JMS
7-4-15	Marched to YPRES 6.45 pm to relieve the French trenches. Relieved them about 11 pm. all quiet.	JMS
8-4-15	Trenches E. of Dyta killed. 2 men wounded	JMS

Army Form C. 2118.

WAR DIARY
or
INTELLIGENCE SUMMARY
(Erase heading not required.)

Instructions regarding War Diaries and Intelligence Summaries are contained in F.S. Regs., Part II. and the Staff Manual respectively. Title pages will be prepared in manuscript.

Hour, Date, Place	Summary of Events and Information	Remarks and references to Appendices
9 – 4 – 15	Trenches. Relieved about 12 mid-night by P.P.C.L.I. Returned to billets at Ypres. 1 man killed, 3 wounded	JW
10 – 4 – 15	In billets at Ypres	JW
11 – 4 – 15	Marched to YPRES 7 pm. Relieved P.P.C.L.I. in same trenches	JW
12 – 4 – 15	Trenches.	JW
13 – 4 – 15	Trenches. Lt. Vincent killed by Sniper. Two men killed, 14 wounded	JW
14 – 4 – 15	Relieved at night by P.P.C.L.I. Two companies bivouacked in huts near BELLEWARDE Lake. Two companies billets in YPRES. 4 men wounded.	JW
15 – 4 – 15	Whole battalion moved up again to POLYGONE Wood about 6 pm in support of a German attack was expected but did not come off.	JW

Army Form C. 2118.

WAR DIARY
or
INTELLIGENCE SUMMARY

(Erase heading not required.)

Instructions regarding War Diaries and Intelligence Summaries are contained in F. S. Regs., Part II. and the Staff Manual respectively. Title pages will be prepared in manuscript.

Hour, Date, Place	Summary of Events and Information	Remarks and references to Appendices
16 – 4 – 15	Remained in support in dug out in POLYGONE WOOD all day. A good deal of German shelling. Lt. Thorpe in dug out left to take over command of 14th Bde. Major Hamilton assumed command	M
17 – 4 – 15	Remained in POLYGONE WOOD Relieved P.P.C.L.I. after dark	M
18 – 4 – 15	Trenches. Heavy firing all round but left actually in front of us. [1 man killed 7 wounded	M
19 – 4 – 15	Trenches. Nothing abnormal. [1 killed, 4 wounded.	M
20 –4 – 15	Trenches. Relieved at night by P.P.C.L.I. Marched through YPRES (which was being heavily bombarded and all troops cleared out) to our bivouac about 1½ miles N.W. of YPRES. 1st Hundred joined us from 5th Fusiliers 1 killed, 1 wounded	M

1247 W 3229 200,000 (E) 8/14 J.B.C. & A.   Forms/C. 2118/11.

Army Form C. 2118.

WAR DIARY or INTELLIGENCE SUMMARY

(Erase heading not required.)

Hour, Date, Place	Summary of Events and Information	Remarks and references to Appendices
21 – 4 – 15	Still in bivouac	
22 – 4 – 15	Orders to fall in came to us & march to POTIJZE Wood. In the evening we were ordered into the reserve in reserve to POTIJZE Wood near Div Hd Qrs. 15 wounded.	
23 – 4 – 15	Remained in POTIJZE Wood till 5 pm then ordered to report to Hd Qrs Canadian Div on YSER CANAL N. of YPRES. A wiring work has been very well done. Orders to take over trenches from K.O.S.B., R.W.K, Y.L.I. who were practically wiped out. The trenches in parts were only knee high but we improved them (Trenches S of & S of PILCHEM FARM) which when 13th Bde. 1 man wounded.	
24 – 4 – 15	Trenches heavily bombarded. Morning. French army to counter attack. Day Reinforced in force. Afternoon the French attack on our D Co's trench running along a hill. We held up our shield in support the French attack. 2 men killed. 17 wounded	

WAR DIARY or INTELLIGENCE SUMMARY

Army Form C. 2118.

(Erase heading not required.)

Instructions regarding War Diaries and Intelligence Summaries are contained in F. S. Regs., Part II. and the Staff Manual respectively. Title pages will be prepared in manuscript.

Hour, Date, Place	Summary of Events and Information	Remarks and references to Appendices
25–4–15	Trenches. Supports found counter attack but failed owing to formation for Heavy bombardment. Reserves ordered to 3 am to move to new trenches in our right. Capt Campbell Maxwell from M.G. wounded. 3 men killed. 9 wounded	m.
26–4–15	Ordered to retire to old trenches. 2nd/4th bombardment taken. Dn. & 2nd Moroccan Dn. counterattacks a failure owing to Germans returning it about 6.7 pm. More troops came up and the attack was launched again. Things for the time not so vigorous but the day. Was when a move was made. Germans to dig in in the night suffered from the guns as we were under fire. 5 men killed. 9 wounded	m.
27–4–15	Moved to new trenches in our right about 1 mile North of WIELTJE, relieved by the Buffs, about 3 hrs we supports to the attack on our left. 1/R. SIRHIND Bde, who had a lot of casualties & advanced a little way in front of us. Heavy bombardment. 7 men killed. 15 wounded	m.

1247 W 3299 200,000 (E) 8/14 J.B.C. & A. Forms/C. 2118/11.

Army Form C. 2118.

WAR DIARY
or
INTELLIGENCE SUMMARY

(Erase heading not required.)

Instructions regarding War Diaries and Intelligence Summaries are contained in F. S. Regs., Part II. and the Staff Manual respectively. Title pages will be prepared in manuscript.

Hour, Date, Place	Summary of Events and Information	Remarks and references to Appendices
28-4-15	Trenches. Heavy howitzer shelling morning and evening. Enemy aeroplane practically put him on the coast by battalion. 2 men killed	nil
29-4-15	Trenches. Quiet day but heavy bombardment in evening. Tried to repulse German attack, were comme- 7 men killed 15 wounded	Trs
30-4-15	Trenches. Terrific bombardment. Enemy lachry- on left to French attack, which J. Williams succeeded. Relieved at night by K.O. Royal Lancaster Regt. marched to HOOGE and orders to bivouac in SANCTUARY Wood under orders of 82nd Bde. 1 man wounded	nil

J.K.M Martin Capt.
Comdg 4th R. Rifle Corps

1247 W 3299 200,000 (E) 8/14 J.B.C. & A. Forms/C. 2118/11.

80th Infantry Brigade.

27th Division.

WAR DIARY

4th BATTN. THE RIFLE BRIGADE.

M A Y

1 9 1 5

80th Infantry Brigade.
27th Division.

WAR DIARY

4th BATTN. THE RIFLE BRIGADE.

M A Y

1 9 1 5

Army Form C. 2118.

INTELLIGENCE SUMMARY

(Erase heading not required.)

Hour, Date, Place	Summary of Events and Information	Remarks and references to Appendices
1 – 5 – 15	Battalion digging in line trench to SANCTUARY WOOD. HOOGE. Capt RPA de Moleyns joins. 3 men wounded.	JMc
2 – 5 – 15	Digging as above	JMc
3 – 5 – 15	Moved to trenches East edge of BELLEWARDE Wood each side of Chateau of HOOGE. The line POLYGONE WOOD was withdrawn for strategic reasons though we Capt Moon Guynn out away sick. Lt Burnell took his adjt 1 man killed 12 wounded	JMc
4 – 5 – 15	Trenches. Germans advanced towards Hooge up Menin Road to our front. Heavily bombarded all day. 2/Lt Greedyan wounded. Germans fired gas shells which had a bad effect in the eyes making them weep & run. Rifle fire. 13 men killed 88 wounded Total Bn 50 missing	JMc
5 – 5 – 15	Trenches. Heavily bombarded. Relieved by 66th at night. 2/Lt Greedyan died from wounds. Capt Cole & Lt Gracey wounded. Went to G H Q line midway morning S of Meenin Rd. 11 men killed and 59 wounded.	JMc

WAR DIARY
or
INTELLIGENCE SUMMARY

(Erase heading not required.)

Army Form C. 2118.

Hour, Date, Place	Summary of Events and Information	Remarks and references to Appendices
6 – 5 – 15	Bivouacking in G.H.Q. line. 2/Lt Duff sent sick.	JMcL.
7 – 5 – 15	As above. Moved to Dugout at BELLEWARDE LAKE near HOOGE at night in support of 60th Bde [?] of [?]. Trenches.	JM
8 – 5 – 15	Heavy german attack on our left. 2/8th Bn. vacates trenches & A Coy. sent to with 2 Bn Dublins. L. to N.E. Corner of BELLEWARDE Wood. L.D. & remr of Bn. moved to in support. B & C sent up in support to P.P.C.L.I. Beginning of day no attempt on The 2/Lt Durant and Woolf killed. Major Hamilton, Captain De Molyneux, Edwards, Acton wounded. 11 men killed, several [?] wounded. Capt. Williamson took over command.	JM
9 – 5 – 15	Trenches. 3 am heavy artillery bombardment followed by german attack from Right to left of BELLEWARDE LAKE. Still stay apart on left but [?] hesitate to open rifle [?] Considerable again & were hit. Leaving to nothing. [?]-[?] 10.10 arrived. Capt Wilkin took M.G. on [?] & commenced B Coy. Lt Pelham Burn went sick. Lt Burnell slightly wounded [?] but not. 30 wounded and 18 missing 9 men killed.	JM

Army Form C. 2118.

WAR DIARY or INTELLIGENCE SUMMARY

(Erase heading not required.)

Instructions regarding War Diaries and Intelligence Summaries are contained in F. S. Regs., Part II. and the Staff Manual respectively. Title pages will be prepared in manuscript.

Hour, Date, Place	Summary of Events and Information	Remarks and references to Appendices
10-5-15	Trenches. Very heavily shelled all day. First trenches & wood vacated by 4KRR and RB owing to shelling. Heavy casualties in A & D Coys who were in first trench. Relieved a 10 p.m. by 1 K.R.R. and 3 K.R.R. (CAVALRY TRENCH) reinforced by no 2 & 3 K.R.R. & 1 A.&S.H. at Tatton. 18 men killed, 10 wounded, 22 missing.	M.
11-5-15	Trenches. Quiet day. German attack made from right without guns against Canadians, nothing much came of it. the wood in front of clearing booked keen. 3 men wounded.	M.
12-5-15	Trenches. Quiet day. Bombardment in evening. Relief by cavalry cancelled, they having to take up position on left. Brigadier General wished us 2 men wounded.	M.
13-5-15	Trenches. 4 a.m. German bombardment commenced and went on till evening, shelling the trenches enough to inflict little trouble. No houses which Bttn H.Q. was in where heavily [?] bombed. Runner & HQ [?] was incapacitation. 2 men killed, 7 men wounded.	M.

1247 W 3299 200,000 (E) 8/14 J.B.C. & A. Forms/C. 2118/11.

WAR DIARY
or
INTELLIGENCE SUMMARY
(Erase heading not required.)

Army Form C. 2118.

Instructions regarding War Diaries and Intelligence Summaries are contained in F. S. Regs., Part II. and the Staff Manual respectively. Title pages will be prepared in manuscript.

Hour, Date, Place	Summary of Events and Information	Remarks and references to Appendices
14–5–15	Trenches. Quiet day. Relieved at night by battalions rttn of 4 KRR and P.P.C.L.I. Have left bivouac near VLAMERTINGHE. about 1 am. 5 men killed 2 wounded.	Casualties 9/5 16 14/5 Killed 21 Wounded 207 Missing 64
15–5–15	Bivouac. Major Gen Snow came to see us. Moved into bivouac near BUSSA BOOM. Draft of 100 men arrived	
16–5–15	As above.	
17–5–15	As above. Capt. Sechiell on 5 days leave. Two report. 7 German prisoners taken with mauser. Rained all day.	
18–5–15	As above. Rained all day. Gen Plumer came to see us.	
19–5–15	As above. M.G. for show came to see us. Cap. Wilson in camp Wave.	
20–5–15	As above. Warm sunny day. F.M. Sir John French inspected the Brigade + congratulated them.	

Army Form C. 2118.

WAR DIARY
or
INTELLIGENCE SUMMARY

(Erase heading not required.)

Instructions regarding War Diaries and Intelligence Summaries are contained in F. S. Regs., Part II. and the Staff Manual respectively. Title pages will be prepared in manuscript.

Hour, Date, Place	Summary of Events and Information	Remarks and references to Appendices
21 – 5 – 15	Still resting in bivouac at BUSSABOOM.	AW
22 – 5 – 15	As above.	AW
23 – 5 – 15	As above. Capt Burrowes & Lt Bourne & Lt Bourne, 2 Lt Kirkpatrick arr. Joined & 1 man.	AW
24 – 5 – 15	As above. At 6 am orders rec'd to move to VLAMERTINGHE YPRES Road in case of emergency, as the 28th Div had been attacked with gas. Reached Q line MENIN ROAD about 8.30 pm & with 3 KRR were ordered to counterattack & help the 84th Bde who were driven in. Came the attack was held up the day wherein in hung the point when the attack stopped. Lieut Bourne killed in HOOGE while on M'cen patrol.	AW
25 – 5 – 15	Remain in same place all day (N.Q MENIN Road about 1500 East of level crossing SE of Ypres). Received orders at dusk to dig a front line & trench about 300 yds forward S of MENIN Road with our left on the road, joining up on the right	AW

1247 W 3299 200,000 (E) 8/14 J.B.C. & A.   Forms/C. 2118/11.

WAR DIARY or INTELLIGENCE SUMMARY

Army Form C. 2118.

Hour, Date, Place	Summary of Events and Information	Remarks and references to Appendices
26-5-15	With 3 KRR & 4th KRR who joined up K & ZOUAVE WOOD. Casualties killed 6 — wounded 50 — missing 6	Among wounded Lyt Major Scott & Lyt Major Pope (since died)
	The new Kemmel all day. Information re HOOGE was reported by us & Germans not definite, but it seems it was finally found on that on that morning the Battn was in ours at St Eloi in by 4th Bn Gordon Highlanders at midnight. Returns to bivouac at BUSSABOOM.	Ms.
27-5-15	In bivouac at BUSSABOOM. Draft of 70 arrived. Chiefly men who had been in the battalion before. The following Officers also joined from 6th B.: Capt. Kennett, 2nd Lt Pigou, 2nd Lt Cowan, 2nd Lt Jennerson, — Mellor, — Naylor.	
28-5-15	In bivouac. Genl Allenby comdg 5th Corps came to say goodbye as Cav. Brigade	Ms

WAR DIARY
or
INTELLIGENCE SUMMARY

(Erase heading not required.)

Instructions regarding War Diaries and Intelligence Summaries are contained in F.S. Regs., Part II. and the Staff Manual respectively. Title pages will be prepared in manuscript.

Army For[m]

Hour, Date, Place	Summary of Events and Information	Remarks and references
29 – 5 – 15	In bivouac. 2/Lt Izard joined from 6th Bn.	Ms.
30 – 5 – 15	In bivouac	Ms.
31 – 5 – 15	Left BUSSABOOM marching as a Brigade at 4.30am arriving at DRANOUTRE about 7.30am where the battalion was in bivouac for the day. 1 man wounded (accidentally)	Ms.

80th Infantry Brigade.

27th Division.

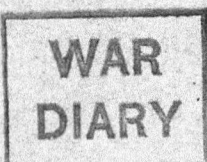

WAR DIARY

4th BATTN. THE RIFLE BRIGADE.

J U N E

1 9 1 5

4th Battalion The Rifle Brigade.

June 1915

1 - 6 - 15   Left DRANOUTRE at 4.45 am arrived at Le Pt MORTIER about 8.30 am, went into billets. General Pulteney Comdg 3rd Corps inspected the Brigade in the road. Some Officers went to inspect the new trenches. 2/Lt Harvey Bathurst joined from A.S.C.

2 - 6 - 15   Left Le Pt MORTIER 3:15 pm arrived ARMENTIERS about 6.30 pm. Relieved 3rd Battn RB & 2 Coys under Capt Burrowes went into support trenches.

3 - 6 - 15   In billets at ARMENTIERS. The same Companies in support as the previous night.

Army Form C. 2118.

WAR DIARY
or
INTELLIGENCE SUMMARY

(Erase heading not required.)

Instructions regarding War Diaries and Intelligence Summaries are contained in F. S. Regs., Part II. and the Staff Manual respectively. Title pages will be prepared in manuscript.

Hour, Date, Place	Summary of Events and Information	Remarks and references to Appendices
4 - 6 - 15	In billets at ARMENTIERS. 2 Lieuts Grant and Morris and draft of 141 other ranks joined 6 Bn.	7ths.
5 - 6 - 15	Into trenches. Relieves P.P.C.L.I and portion of K.S.L.I	7th.
6 - 6 - 15	Trenches. 2 Lieut Auisiault 6th Bn joined.	7th.
7 - 6 - 15	Trenches. Wounded 2.	7th.
8 - 6 - 15	Trenches. 2nd Lieuts Temperley & Currach 6th Bn joined. Killed 1. Wounded 2.	7th.
9 - 6 - 15	Trenches. 2 Lt Lurie returns from machine gun course. Wounded 1.	7th.
10 - 6 - 15	Trenches	7th.
11 - 6 - 15	Trenches. Relieved in evening. Killed 1. Wounded 1.	7th.

Army Form C. 2118.

WAR DIARY
or
INTELLIGENCE SUMMARY

(Erase heading not required.)

Instructions regarding War Diaries and Intelligence Summaries are contained in F. S. Regs., Part II. and the Staff Manual respectively. Title pages will be prepared in manuscript.

Hour, Date, Place	Summary of Events and Information	Remarks and references to Appendices
12 – 6 – 15	In Billets in Armentières	JHS
13 – 6 – 15	as above.	JHS
14 – 6 – 15	Relieved K.S.L.I. in trenches	JHS
15 – 6 – 15	In trenches	JHS
16 – 6 – 15	Trenches. wounded 2.	JHS
17 – 6 – 15	Trenches. 2/Lt Henderson went sick.	JHS
18 – 6 – 15	Trenches. Luminous of Battle of Waterloo. Quite quiet.	JHS
19 – 6 – 15	Trenches. 2/Lt Huttle from 5th Bn as 7o Star rank arrived	JHS
20 – 6 – 15	Trenches. 2/Lt Mirick from 5th Bn joins. Relieved by 3 KRR in K.S.L.I. Killed 2. wounded 1. Driver to hospital 1. C Coy & half of A remain in support	JHS

1247 W 3299 200,000 (E) 8/14 J.B.C. & A.   Forms/C. 2118/11.

WAR DIARY
or
INTELLIGENCE SUMMARY

Army Form C. 2118.

(Erase heading not required.)

Hour, Date, Place	Summary of Events and Information	Remarks and references to Appendices
21 - 6 - 15	In Wilds. Battalion held in reserve in c/c 5 pm.	JHS
22 - 6 - 15	As above. B Coy relieved C in support.	JHS
23 - 6 - 15	Relieved 3 KRR in trenches. B Coy 6th Queens (new army) attached for instruction.	JHS
24 - 6 - 15	Trenches. Left hand shell is now mine. Lt Montenyoye done heavy rain in afternoon. Mountain gun fires on dug hues in evening, wounding 2.	JHS
25 - 6 - 15	Trenches. More rain. Sappers mining chimneys much. A Coy had. 17 Canadian Cadets joined for one day's instruction. 2/Lt Fairbrass Ross and 64 other ranks joined.	JHS
26 - 6 - 15	Trenches. Mountain gun again fired.	JHS
27 - 6 - 15	Relieved in evening by D.C.L.I. & 2 w/ Border. We had men in the trenches we were in.	JHS

Army Form C. 2118.

WAR DIARY
or
INTELLIGENCE SUMMARY
(Erase heading not required.)

Instructions regarding War Diaries and Intelligence Summaries are contained in F. S. Regs., Part II. and the Staff Manual respectively. Title pages will be prepared in manuscript.

Hour, Date, Place	Summary of Events and Information	Remarks and references to Appendices
28 - 6 - 15	2 Platoons in Annexation.	in
29 - 6 - 15	As above. Two shells, wounded to be ready to be sent with the open. 2/Lt Henderson returned from hospital	in
30 - 6 - 15	As above.	in

80th Infantry Brigade.
27th Division.

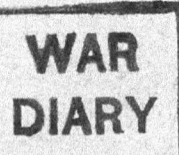

4th BATT. THE RIFLE BRIGADE.

J U L Y

1 9 1 5

Army Form C. 2118.

WAR DIARY
or
INTELLIGENCE SUMMARY

(Erase heading not required.)

Instructions regarding War Diaries and Intelligence Summaries are contained in F. S. Regs., Part II. and the Staff Manual respectively. Title pages will be prepared in manuscript.

Hour, Date, Place	Summary of Events and Information	Remarks and references to Appendices
1 - 7 - 15	Returned to trenches relieving 3 KRR. Killed 1.	JHW.
2 - 7 - 15	Trenches. Draft of arrived, also ten men drafts from 9th Lancers. Wounded 2 (1 died)	JHW.
3 - 7 - 15	Trenches. Enemy guns active in morning, in particular against an aeroplane.	JHW.
4 - 7 - 15	Trenches.	JHW.
5 - 7 - 15	Trenches. Rather more shelling, enemy had prepared searchlight from their support trench. Relieved by K.S.L.I. at night. Killed 1. Wounded 6.	JHW.
6 - 7 - 15	In billets at Armentières. 1 9th the other 2 wounds	JHW
7 - 7 - 15	Relieved 3 KRR in trenches at night.	JHW

Army Form C. 2118.

WAR DIARY
or
INTELLIGENCE SUMMARY

(Erase heading not required.)

Instructions regarding War Diaries and Intelligence Summaries are contained in F. S. Regs., Part II. and the Staff Manual respectively. Title pages will be prepared in manuscript.

Hour, Date, Place	Summary of Events and Information	Remarks and references to Appendices
8 – 7 – 15	Trenches. Capt Gathorne Hardy joined & took over Command. Wounded 3.	Ams.
9 – 7 – 15	Relieved at night by 3 KRR. went into billets in the Asylum Armentières.	Ms.
10 – 7 – 15	Shells in the Asylum in the morning. Wounded 2	Ams.
11 – 7 – 15	In billets. 2 men rejoined to bomb.	Ams.
12 – 7 – 15	as above	Ams.
13 – 7 – 15	Relieve 4th KRR in trenches Epinette	Ms.
14 – 7 – 15	Trenches quiet	Ms.
15 – 7 – 15	Trenches. Shelling in evening. 1 killed. 8 wounded.	Ms.
16 – 7 – 15	Relieved by Border Regt 4/5 + 7/5 Fusiliers to trench. marches	Ams.

1247 W 3299 200,000 (E) 8/14 J.B.C. & A. Forms/C. 2118/11.

WAR DIARY
or
INTELLIGENCE SUMMARY

(Erase heading not required.)

Army Form C. 2118.

Hour, Date, Place	Summary of Events and Information	Remarks and references to Appendices
17-7-15	to billets near Steenwerck, a very wet night and a long relief	JM
18-7-15	Arris at Steenwerck, the same	JM
19-7-15	at rest at above. wounded 1 (shot by accident)	JM
20-7-15	ditto	JM
21-7-15	Mons Kruen Enquiry men given in	JM
22-7-15	Refitting etc as above	MJM
31-7-15	do	MJM

80th Infantry Brigade.
27th Division.

WAR DIARY

4th BATTN. THE RIFLE BRIGADE.

A U G U S T

1 9 1 5

WAR DIARY
or
INTELLIGENCE SUMMARY

(Erase heading not required.)

Army Form C. 2118.

Instructions regarding War Diaries and Intelligence Summaries are contained in F.S. Regs, Part II. and the Staff Manual respectively. Title pages will be prepared in manuscript.

Hour, Date, Place	Summary of Events and Information	Remarks and references to Appendices
1. 5. 15	In billets Gauinghem	J.M.N.
2. 5. 15	Moved into billets l'Armée. Brigade Reserve.	M.H.
5. 5. 15	1 Co. Support in Bois-Grenier line.	
9. 5. 15	Relieved K.S.L.I. in trenches near Bois-Grenier	J.M.N.
15. 5. 15	9.5.15. 1 Killed.	
	10.5.15 1 wounded	
	13.5.15. 2 R.M. wounded 2/Lt. Anderson wounded. 20 Bath	
	14.5.15. 2/Lt. Henderson wounded	
	15.5.15 2 wounded	
	16.5.15. 2 R.M. wounded. Captain R.P. Burrowes wounded	
16.5.15 to 22nd	Moved into billets ½ mile North of Gm's Pot. 1 Co. Support in Bois Grenier line	J.M.N.
23rd	Relieved KSLI in trenches Bois-Grenier	
24th 29 M.H 30 hr.	In trenches 25.5.15. 2 killed. 6 wounded	
	26.5.15. 1 " 1 "	
	27.5.15. 1 " 3 "	
	ENQVINGHEM ⎰ 28.5.15. 1 " " "	
	⎱ 29.5.15. " " 3 "	
	30.5.15. 1 " " "	
30/5 – 31/5	Moved into billets	

1247 W 3299 200,000 (E) 8/14 J.B.C. & A. Forms/C. 2118/11."

80th Infantry Brigade.
27th Division.

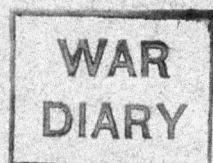

4th BATTN. THE RIFLE BRIGADE.

S E P T E M B E R

1 9 1 5

Army Form C. 2118.

INTELLIGENCE SUMMARY

(Erase heading not required.)

Instructions regarding War Diaries and Intelligence Summaries are contained in F. S. Regs., Part II. and the Staff Manual respectively. Title pages will be prepared in manuscript.

Hour, Date, Place	Summary of Events and Information	Remarks and references to Appendices
1.9.15 – 13.9.15	Billets near ERQUINGHAM	
14.9.15	The Battn paraded at 6.35 p.m. & marched to Borre arriving at billets 2. a.m. 15th.	
17.9.15	The Brigade was inspected by Lt. General Pulteney on 16th. Brigade leaving 3rd Corps.	
18.9.15	The Battn entrained at HAZEBROUCK at 3.06 p.m. for VILLAUCOURT.	
19.9.15	Arrived GUILLAUCOURT at 4 a.m. & detrained an hour later. March to FOISSEY 1 mile south of BRAY & went into huts.	
20.9.15	Battn moved to CAPPY in support.	
25.9.15	Battn relieved K.S.L.I in trenches East of CAPPY & came out on 1 Oct.	Sept. 26th 1 man wounded. 27th 2/Lt T. Fairfax Ros Wounded. 28th 1 man wounded. 1st 3 men wounded (actually) 1 man wounded
30.9.15	2 Companies to Scottish Rifles attached for instruction for 2 days	

80th Infantry Brigade.
27th Division.

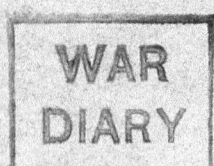

4th BATTN. THE RIFLE BRIGADE.

O C T O B E R

1 9 1 5

Army Form C. 2118.

WAR DIARY
or
INTELLIGENCE SUMMARY

(Erase heading not required.)

Instructions regarding War Diaries and Intelligence Summaries are contained in F. S. Regs., Part II. and the Staff Manual respectively. Title pages will be prepared in manuscript.

Hour, Date, Place	Summary of Events and Information	Remarks and references to Appendices
Oct. 1.	Batln in billets moved into billets at CAPPY relieved by K.S.L.I.	JJH
" 5	Batln relieved K.S.L.I. in trenches	JJH
" 6	2 Companies 2 Devonshire Regt attached for 2 days.	JJH
" 9	1 man wounded. Batln relieved by K.S.L.I. and moved into billets at FROISSEY.	DJH
" 13	Batln relieved K.S.L.I. in trenches.	DJH
" 16	Batln relieved by 7Bn. S.W.Borders, moved into divisional reserve at PROYART.	JJH
" 20	Batln moved into Bde Reserve at CAPPY.	NJH
" 22	Batln relieved K.S.L.I. in trenches	NJH
" 25	Relieved by 119 French Regt. and went into billets at CAPPY	NJH
" 26	Marched to MORCOURT about 6½ miles	JJH
" 27	" " BOVES (under canvas) about 14 miles	JJH
"	" " CLAIRY about 10 miles.	NJH

www.ingramcontent.com/pod-product-compliance
Lightning Source LLC
Chambersburg PA
CBHW081243170426
43191CB00034B/2021